I0457134

TRACING NUMBERS

ASL Handwriting Book

www.mamaishere.com

Copyright © 2022 Writerverse Journey. All rights reserved. Personal use only.

"We must find time to stop and thank the people who make a difference in our lives."
- John F. Kennedy

So, I would like to say: THANK YOU!

Hi! I used to be a nanny when I was a teenager, then a tutor and a teacher (at the same time I got my Bachelor's Degree in Design) . Nowadays, I am a designer and a mom - or how I like to call it: mama). This is how "Mama Is Here" was born!

I hope I am making a difference in your children's lives and thank you for making one in mine!

@mamaishere2021

follow to check daily activities you can do with your little one!

Text and illustration © Copyright 2022 Writerverse Journey
Book Design by Kelle Lima a.k.a. Mama Is Here

ISBN: 979-8-9857051-3-3

Published in 2022 by Writerverse Journey LLC, in Salt Lake City, UT, USA. All rights reserved.

No part of this book may be reproduced or used in any manner without written permission of the copyright owner. For more information email 'writerversejourney@gmail.com'

Dear Teachers & Parents,

This pencil control book contains numbers from 0 to 10 along with American Sign Language support.

It is recommended that you are an active part of the learning process: help the child learn, count the objects with them, praise their improvement, don't do long sessions, and try working on lessons when the kid is not feeling tired.

I hope I'm providing your kid the ability to count, recognize and write numbers, and their respective signs (hand gestures)!

Thank you again and have fun!

Cheers,
Kelle Lima

Check out other books from "Little Fingers" collection, such as:

TRACING LETTERS:
ASL Handwriting Book

ZERO

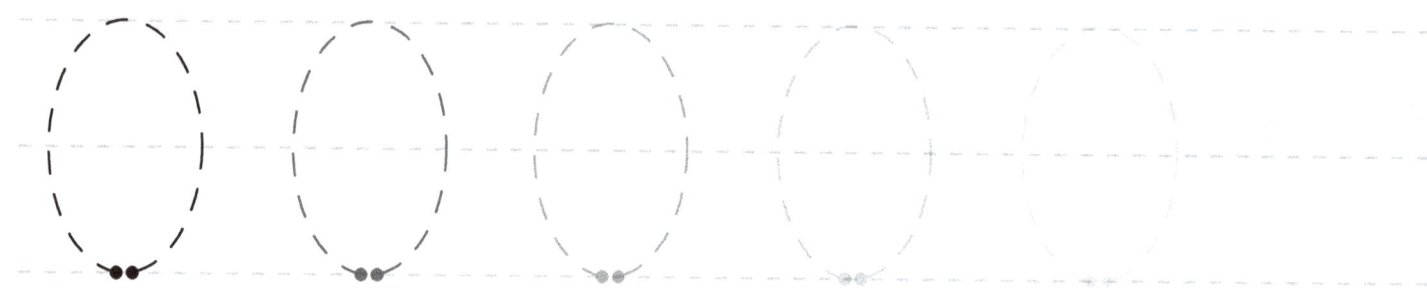

Find and (circle) the number 0!

Paint the number 0!

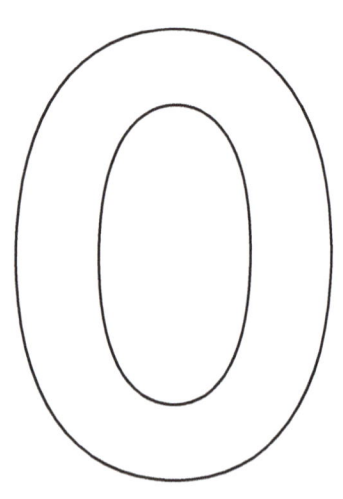

Let's practice number 0 now! Remember: around

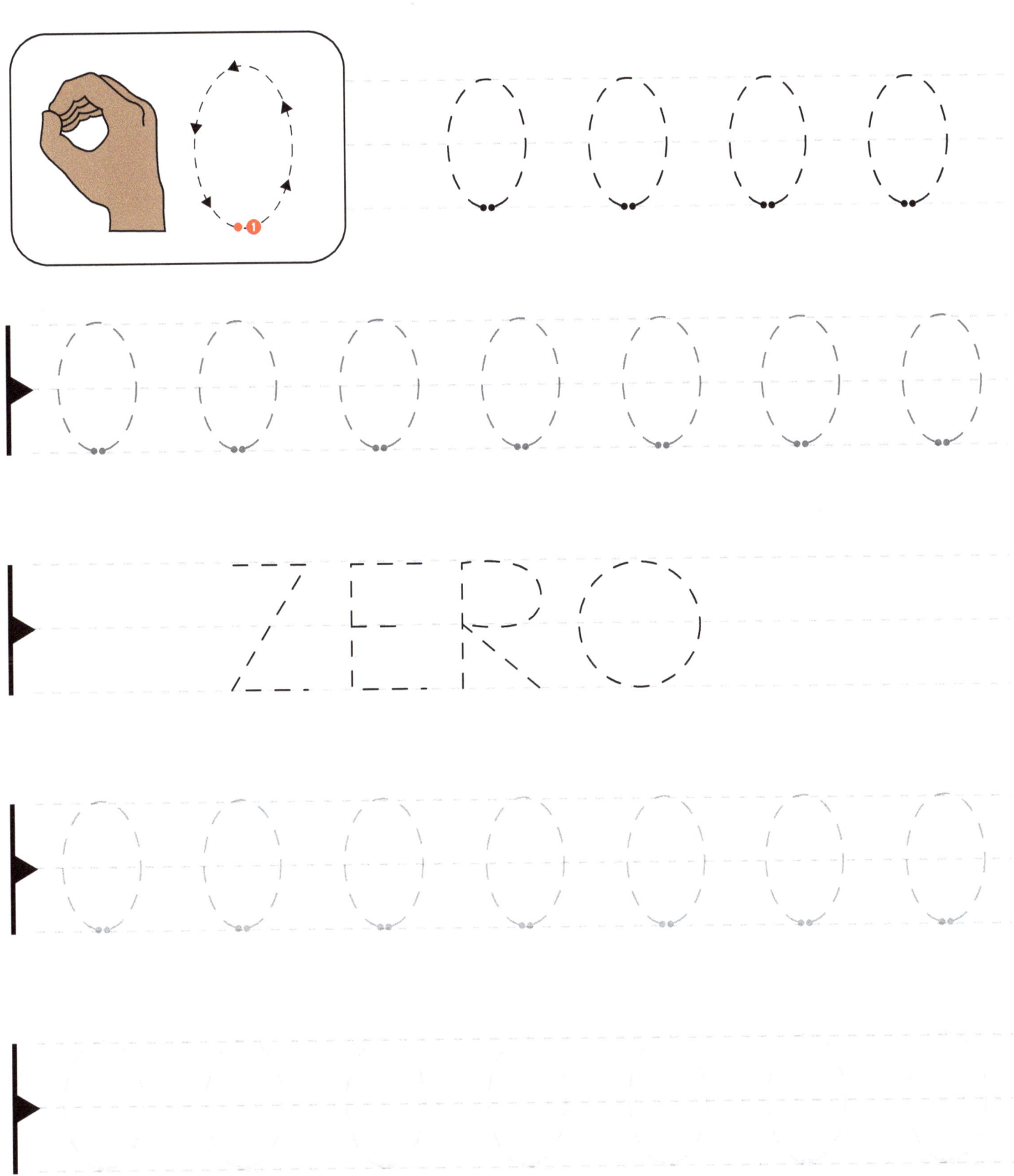

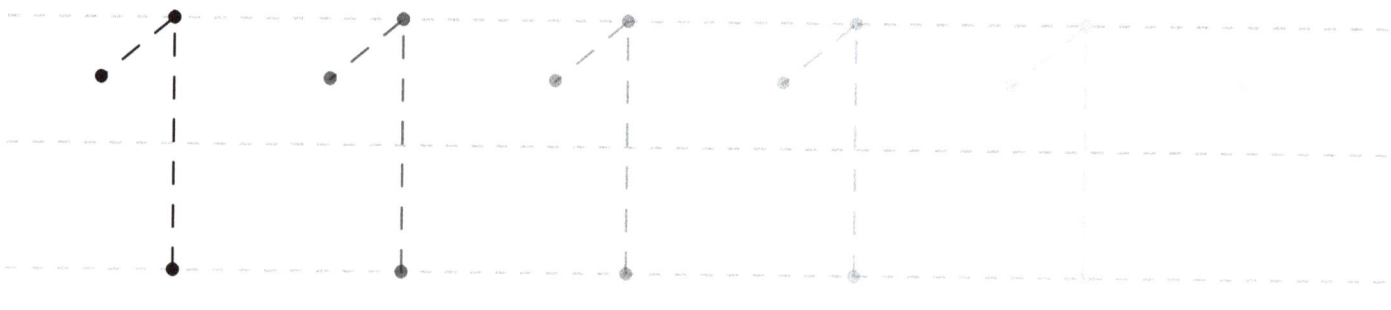

Trace 1 candle!

Color 1 sun:

Let's practice number 1 now! Remember: over-slant-down

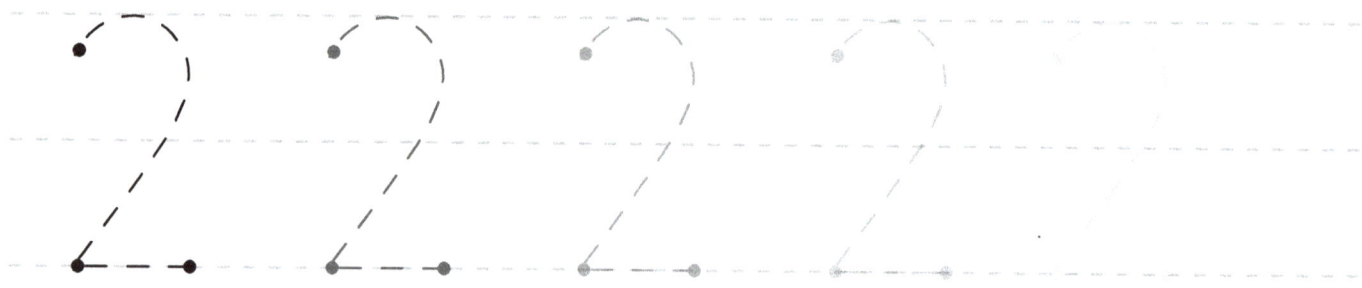

Trace the other half of each heart. How many hearts do you see?

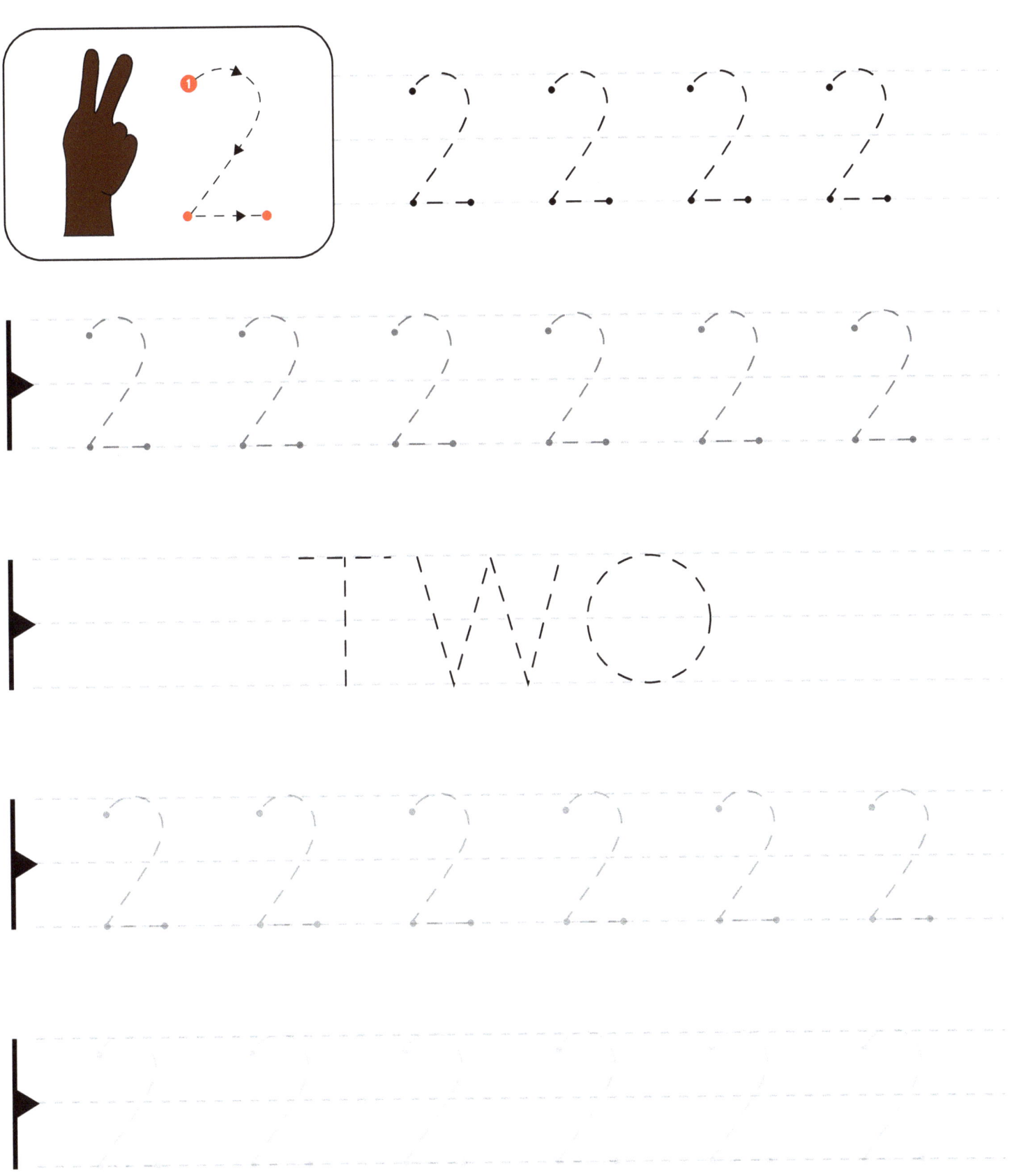

THREE

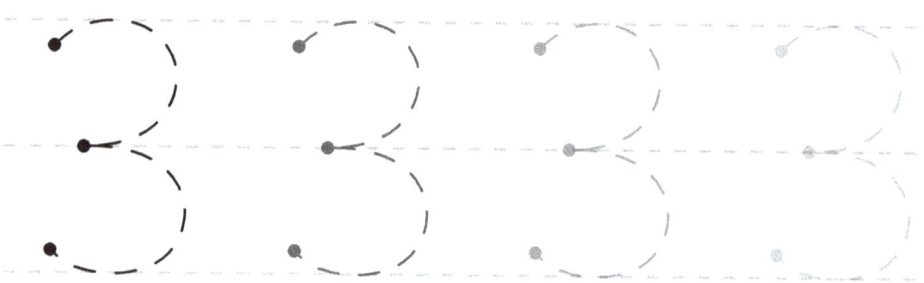

Feed 3 spoons of food to the baby?

Let's practice number 3 now! Remember: roll-roll

FOUR

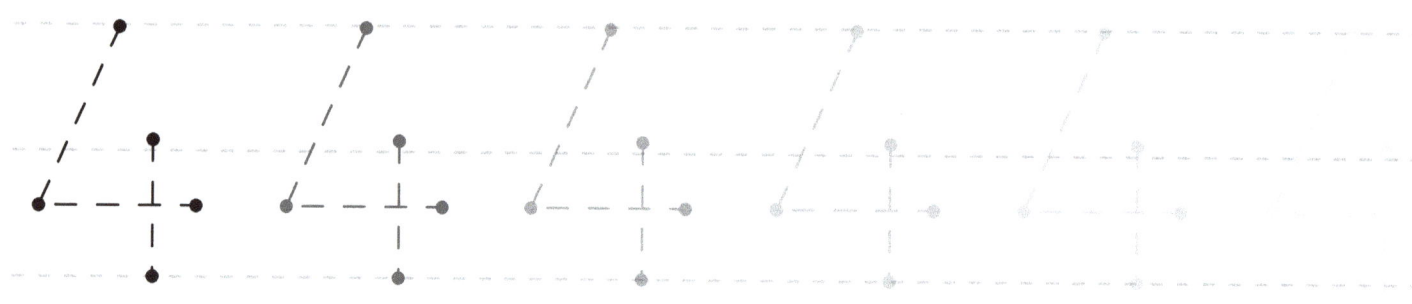

Trace the 4 squares. How many sides does each square have?

Find and (circle) all the fours?

4 5 2 4
3 8 9 1 6
7 4 0 4

Let's practice number 4 now! Remember: down-over-lift-down

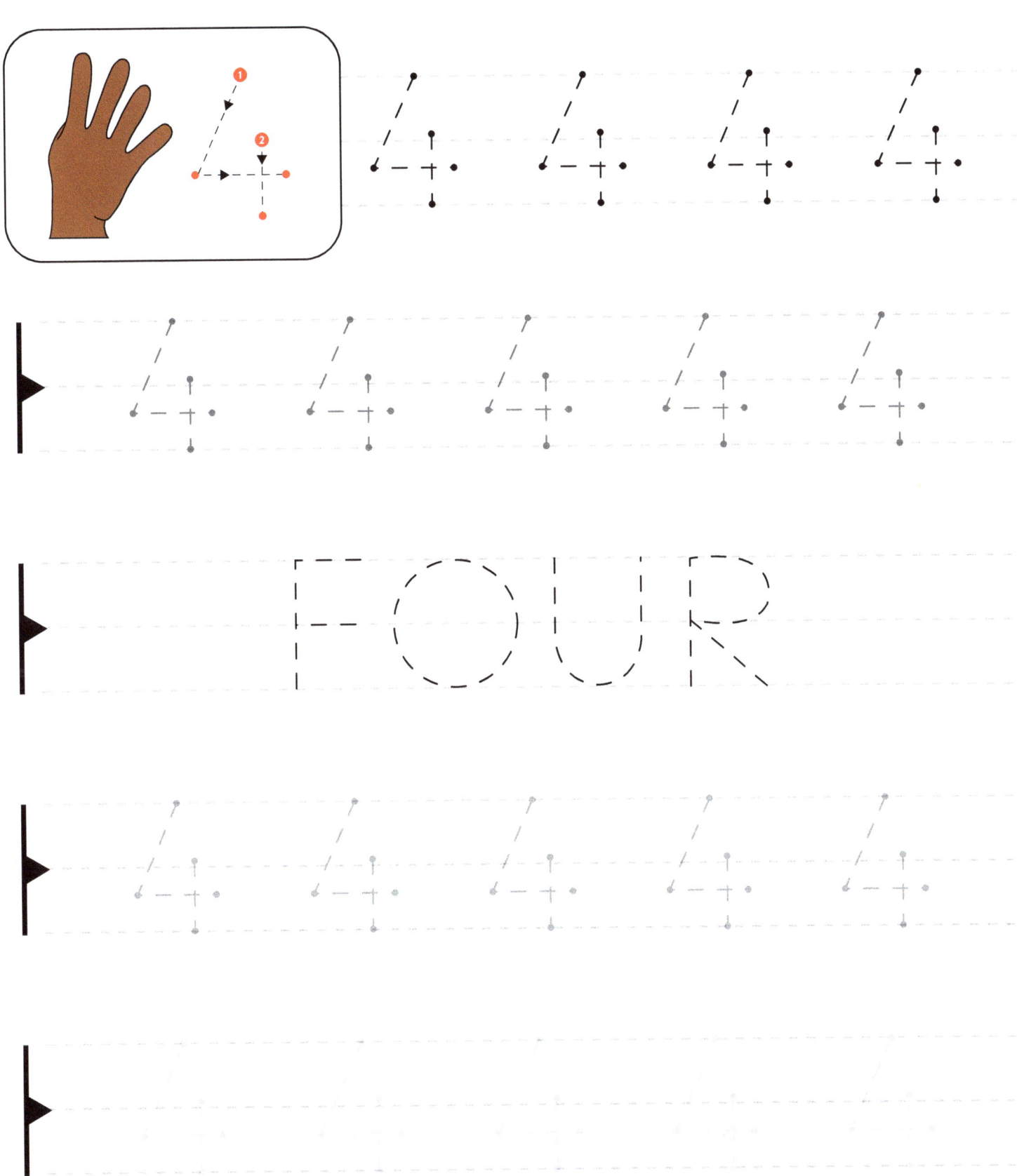

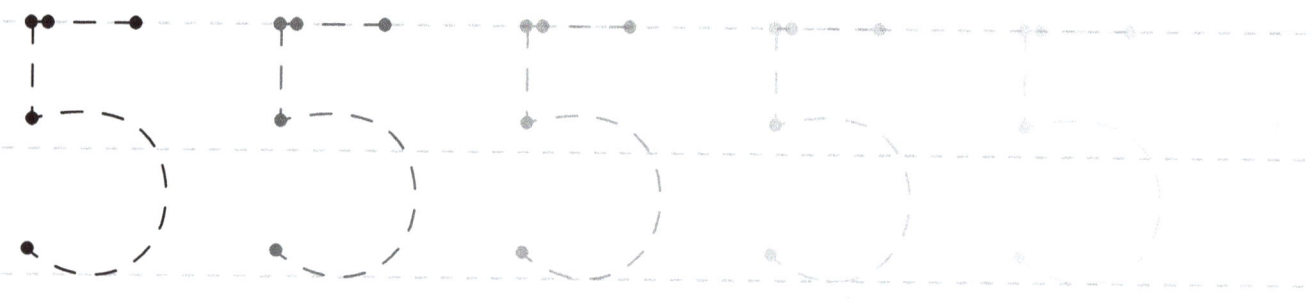

Give me a high 5!

Trace the 5 point of the star.

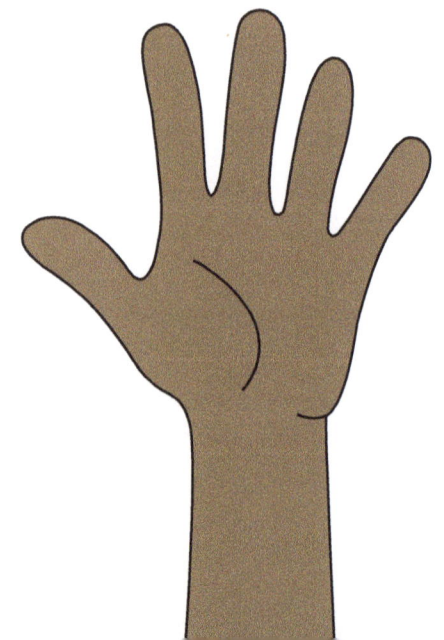

Let's practice number 5 now! Remember: down-roll-lift-over

SIX

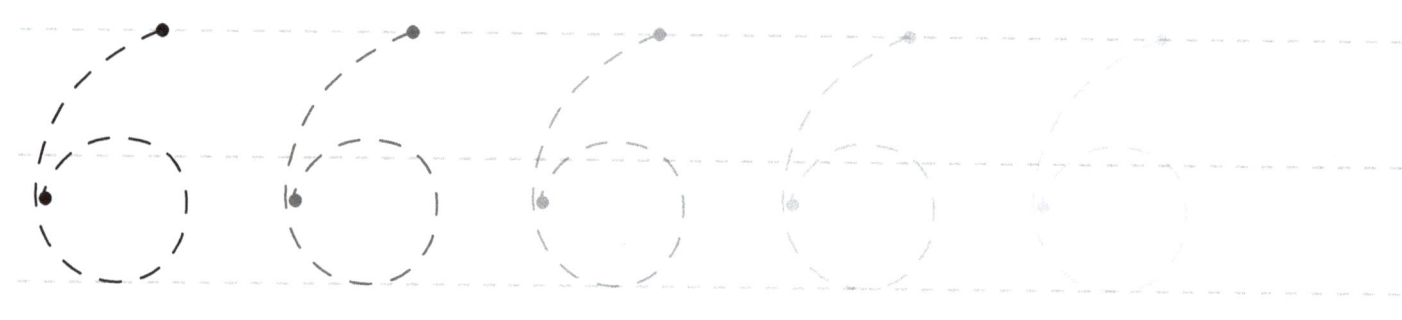

Connect the 6 hexagons:

How many slices of pizza do you see?

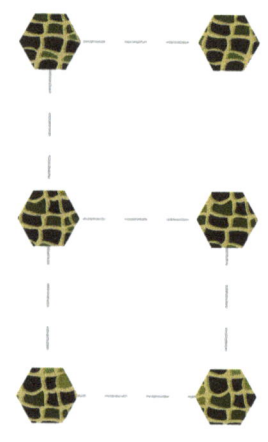

Let's practice number 6 now! Remember: roll down-around

SEVEN

Color the 7 colors the rainbow below!

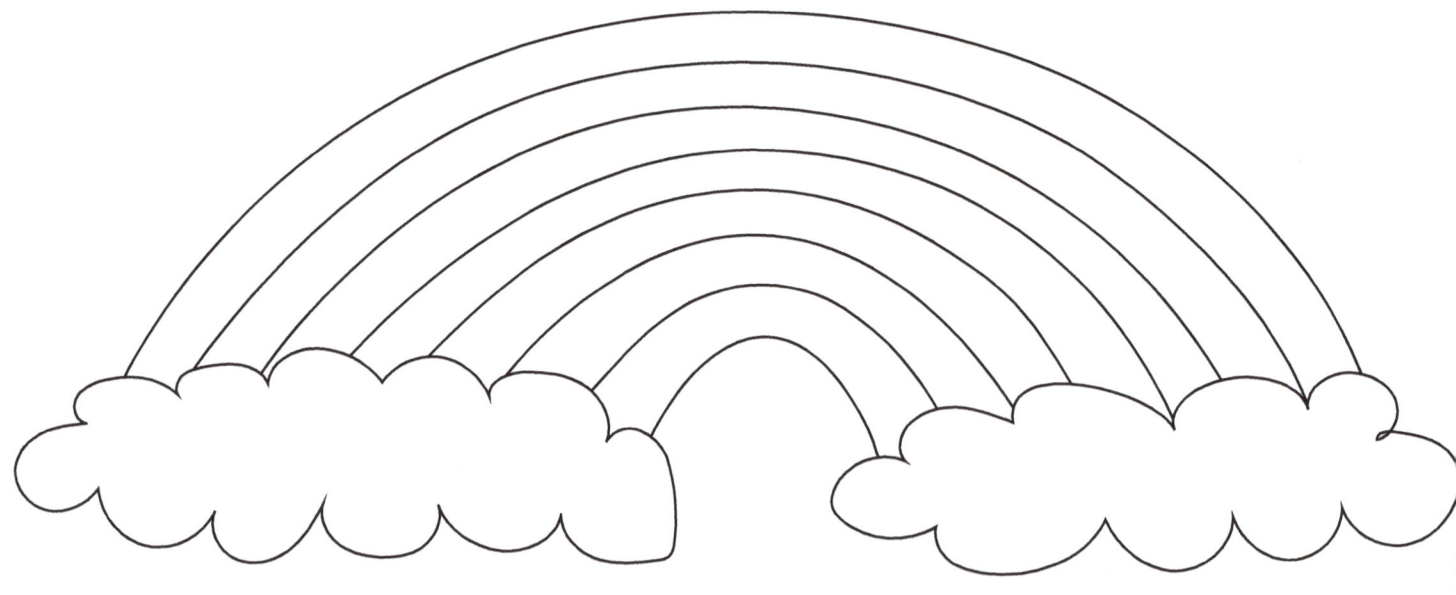

EIGHT

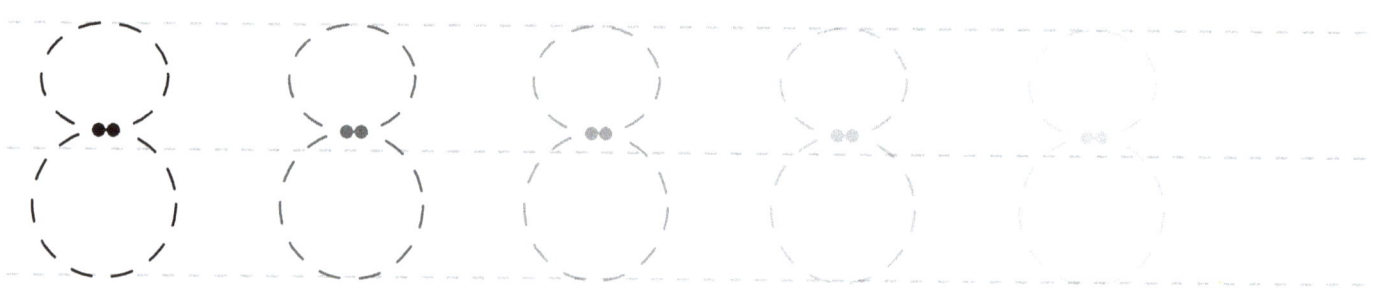

Paint the 8 parts of the octopus that are blank!

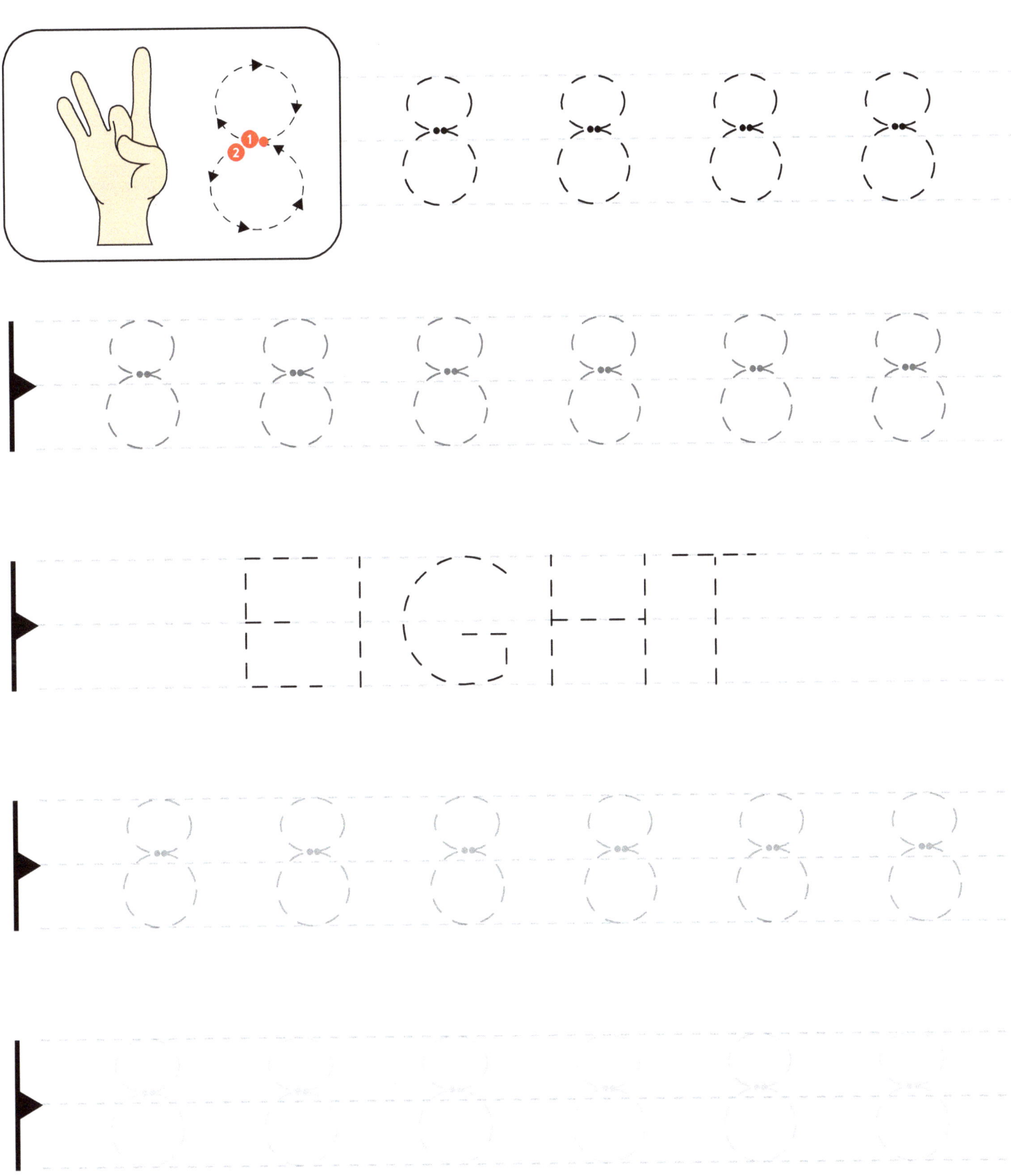

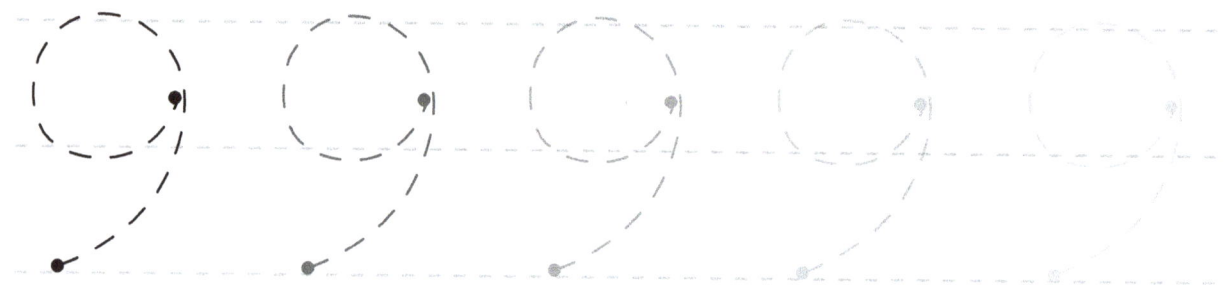

Press the channel 9!

Paint the 9 circles below:

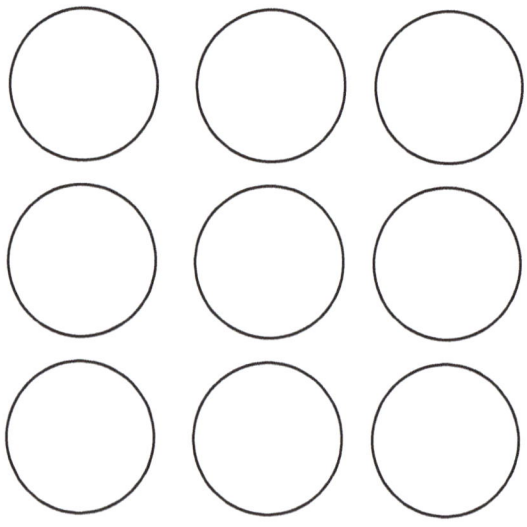

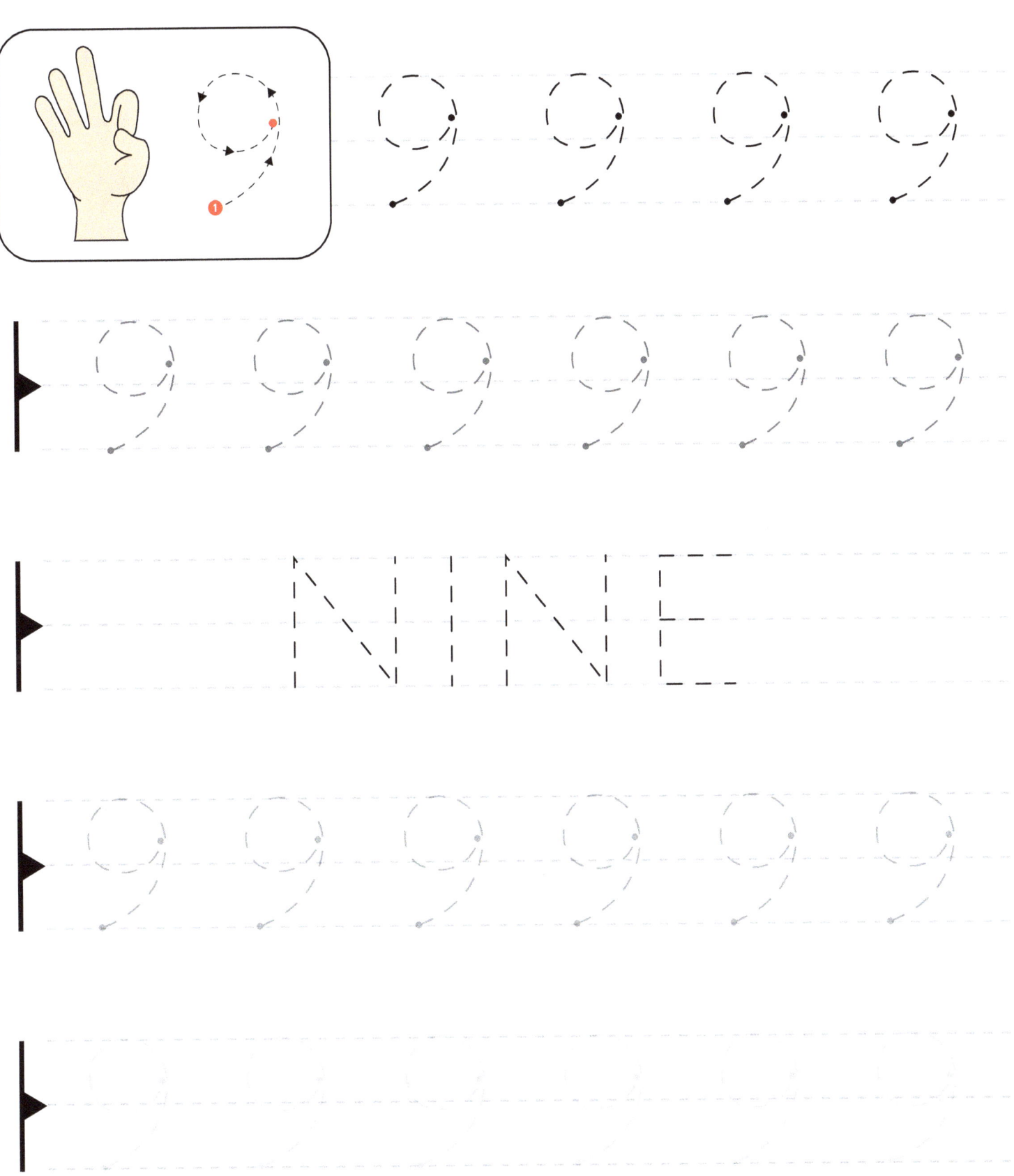

TEN

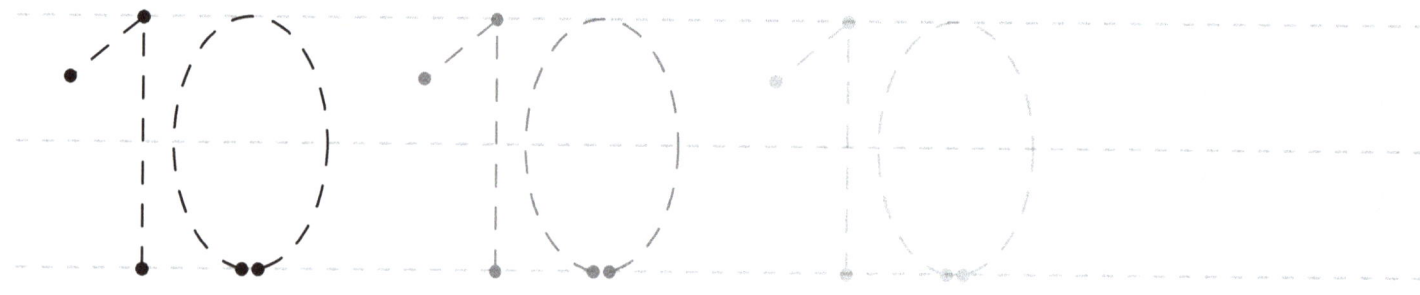

Give 10 bananas to the monkey!

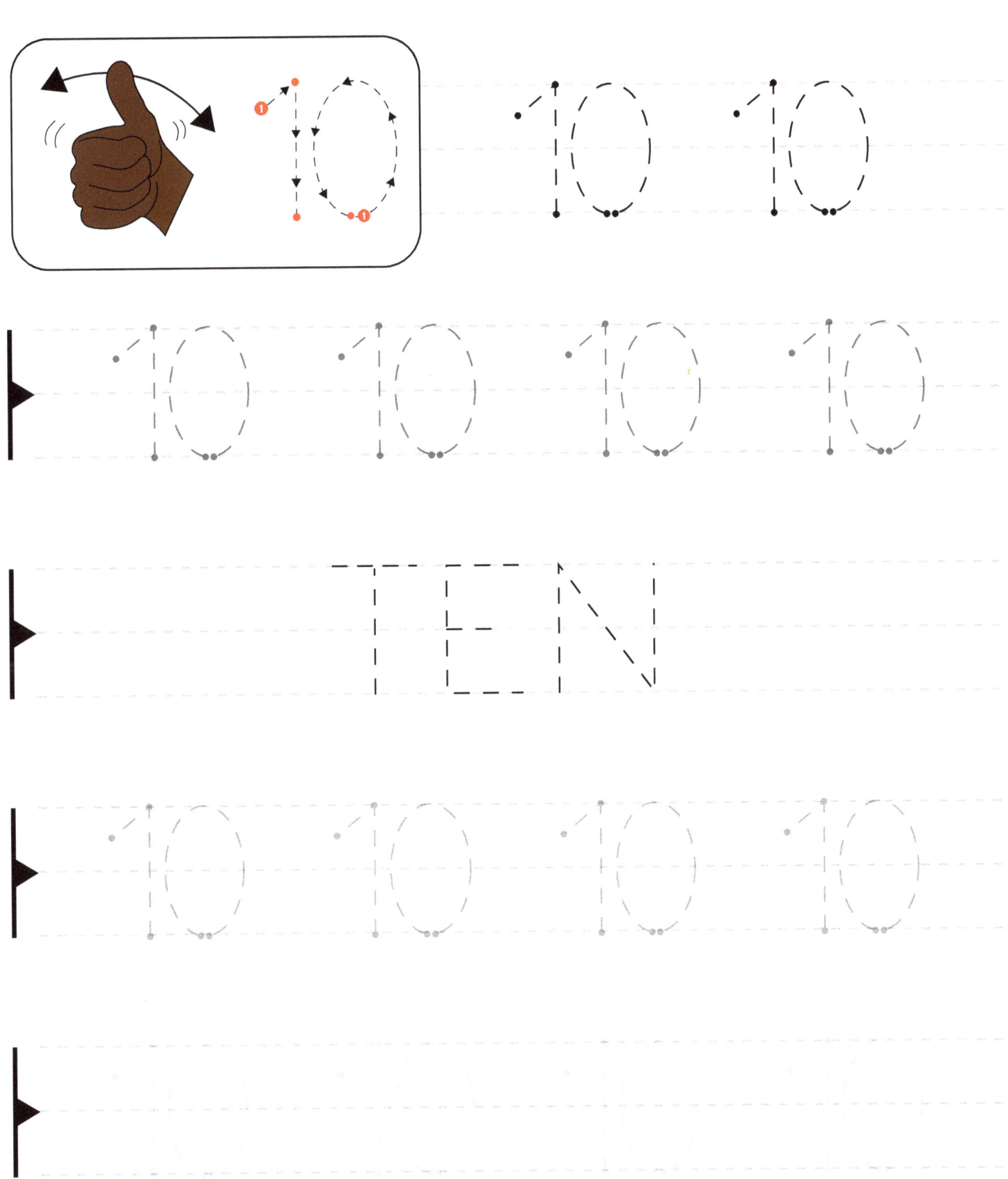

Match the numbers and the hands below!

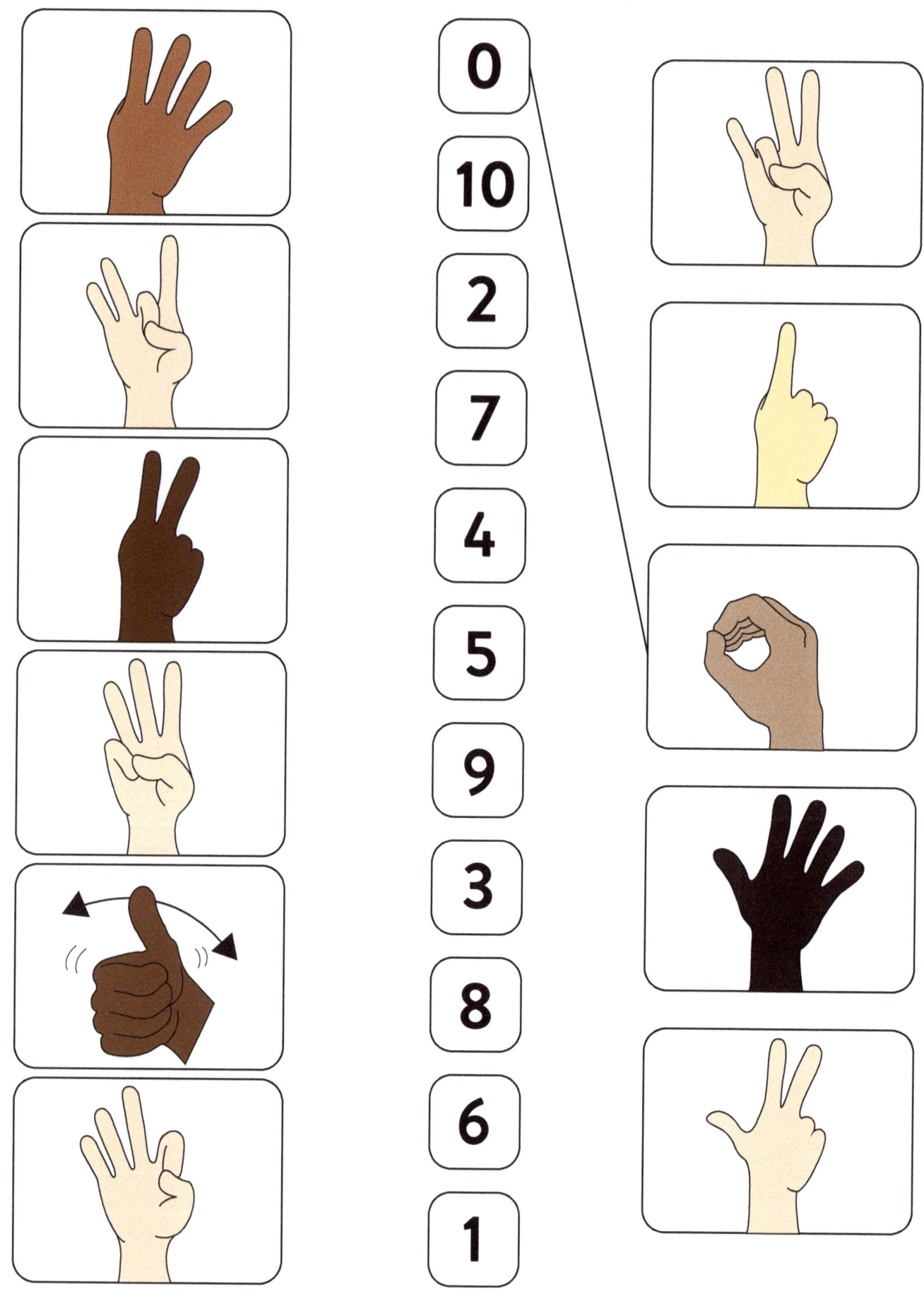

Trace the numbers and complete the images!

Paint the number of stars that is asked!

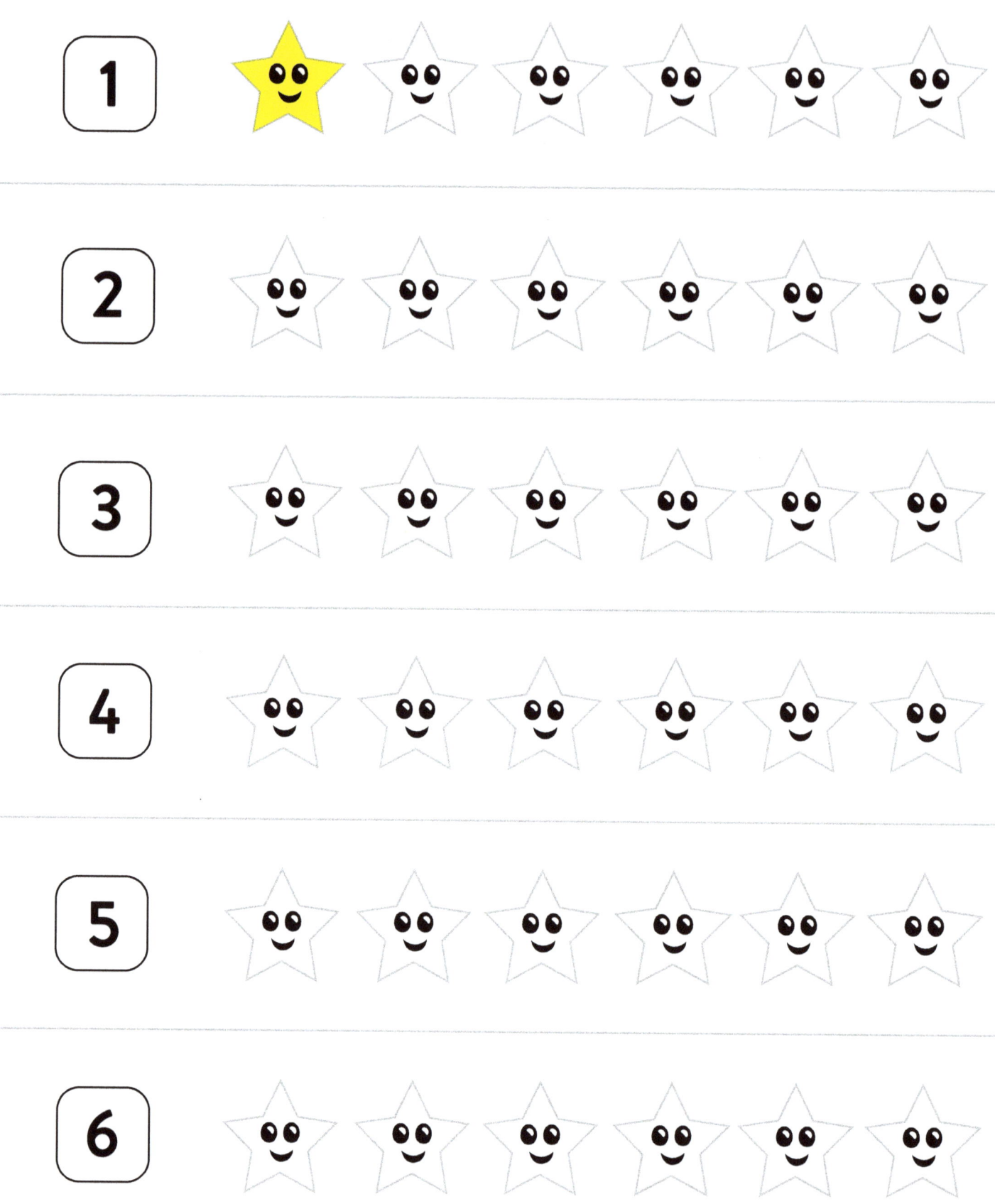

Match the numbers and the Words

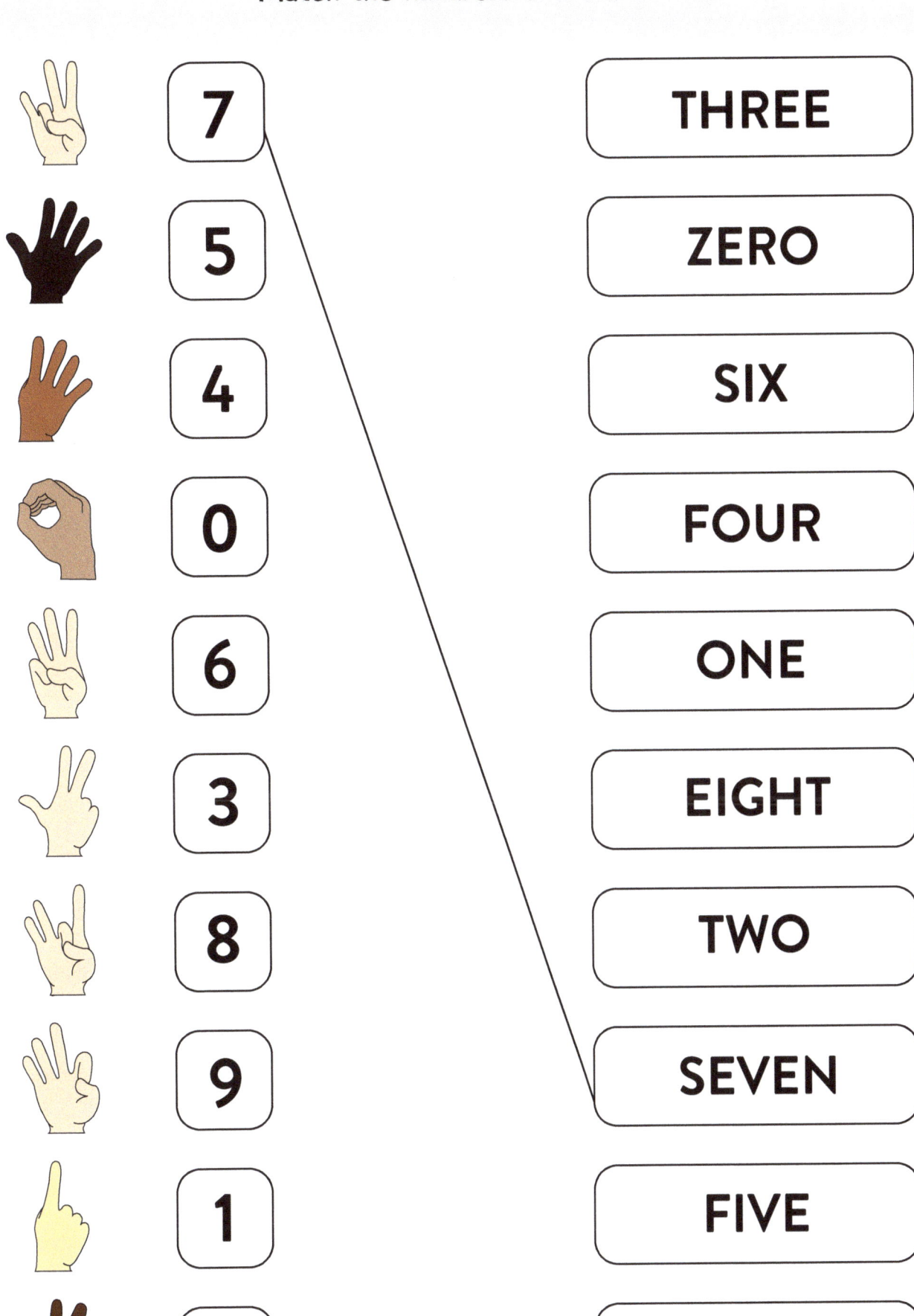

Can you paint the 6 yellow dots in each piece below?

Can you draw 8 in the aquarium below?

Write the missing numbers!

Match the number to the group of birds?

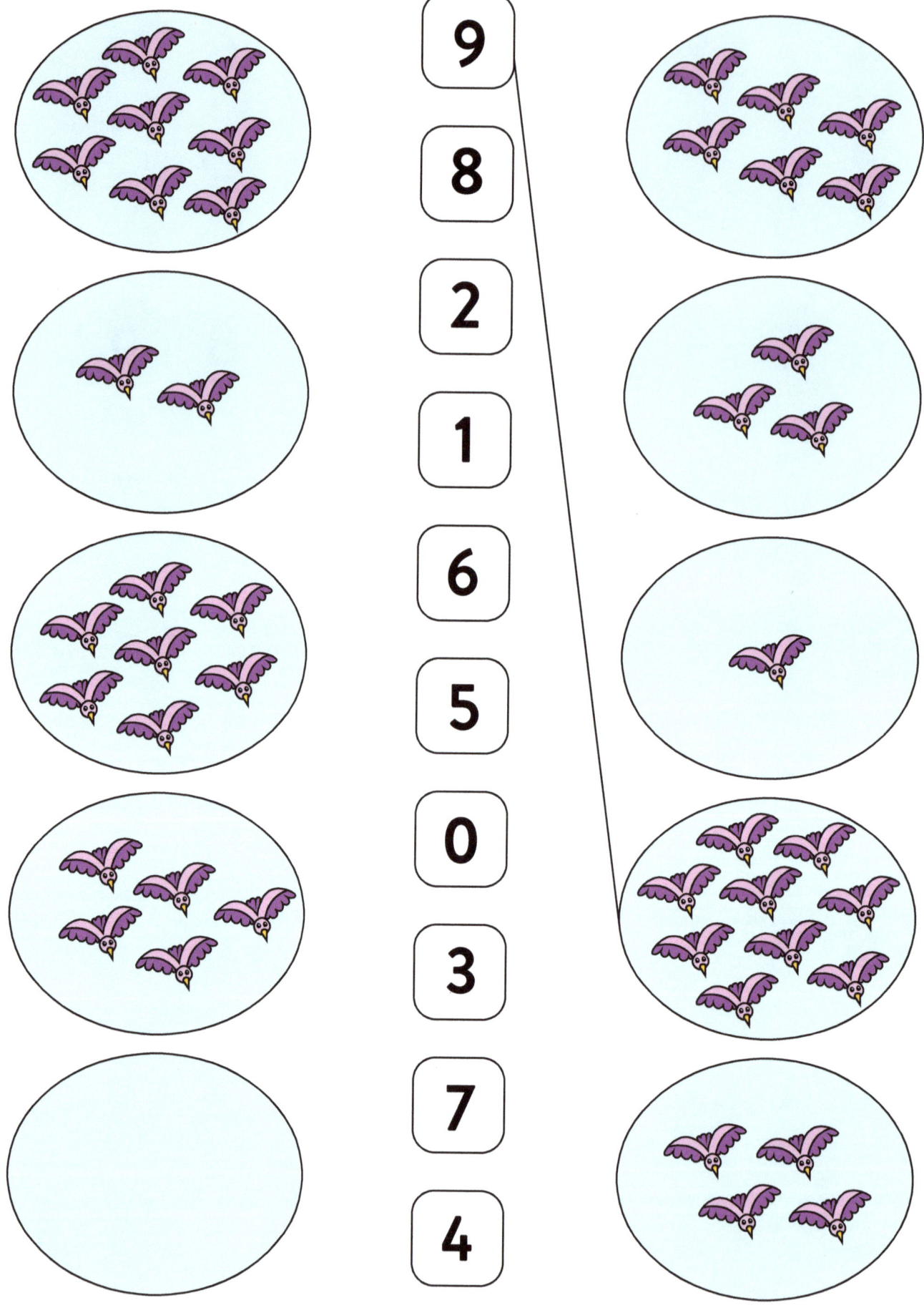

Review "roll" ⟲ skill by tracing their ears below!

Now that you practiced roll, trace the numbers below

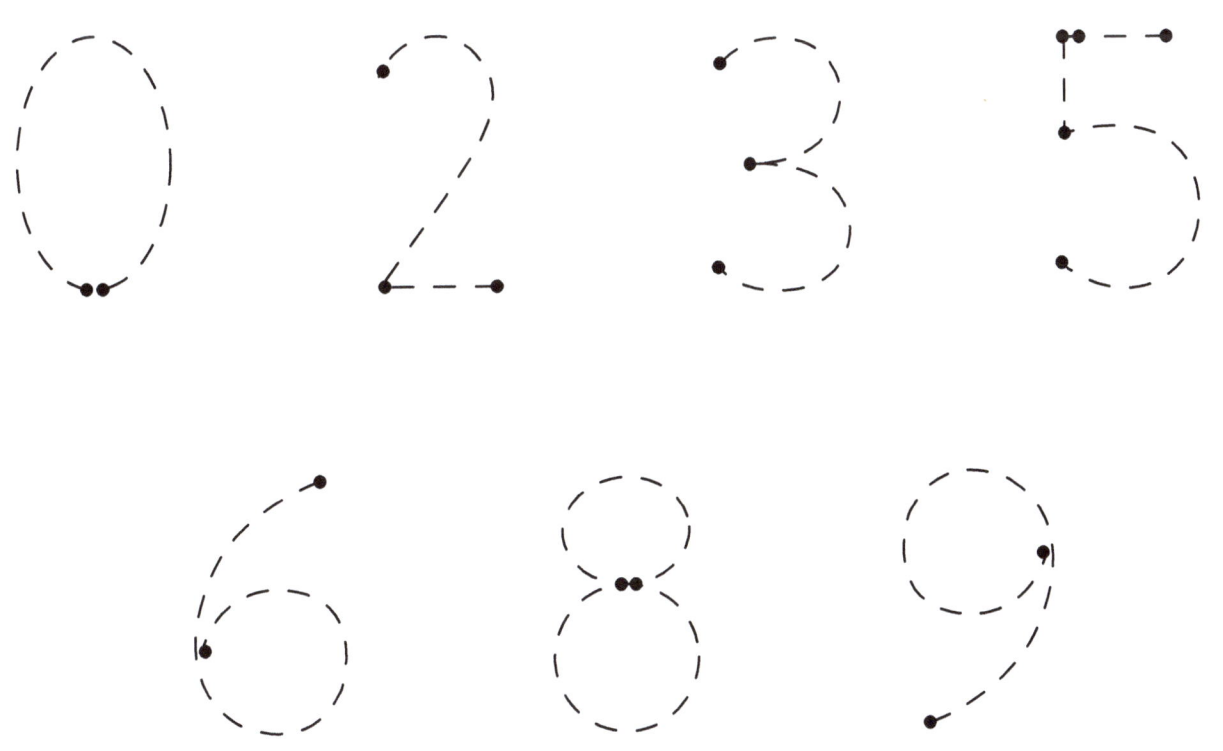

Trace the 5 on the seahorse. How many bubbles do you see?

Can you find and (circle) the group of 3 flowers?

Match the numbers and the Words

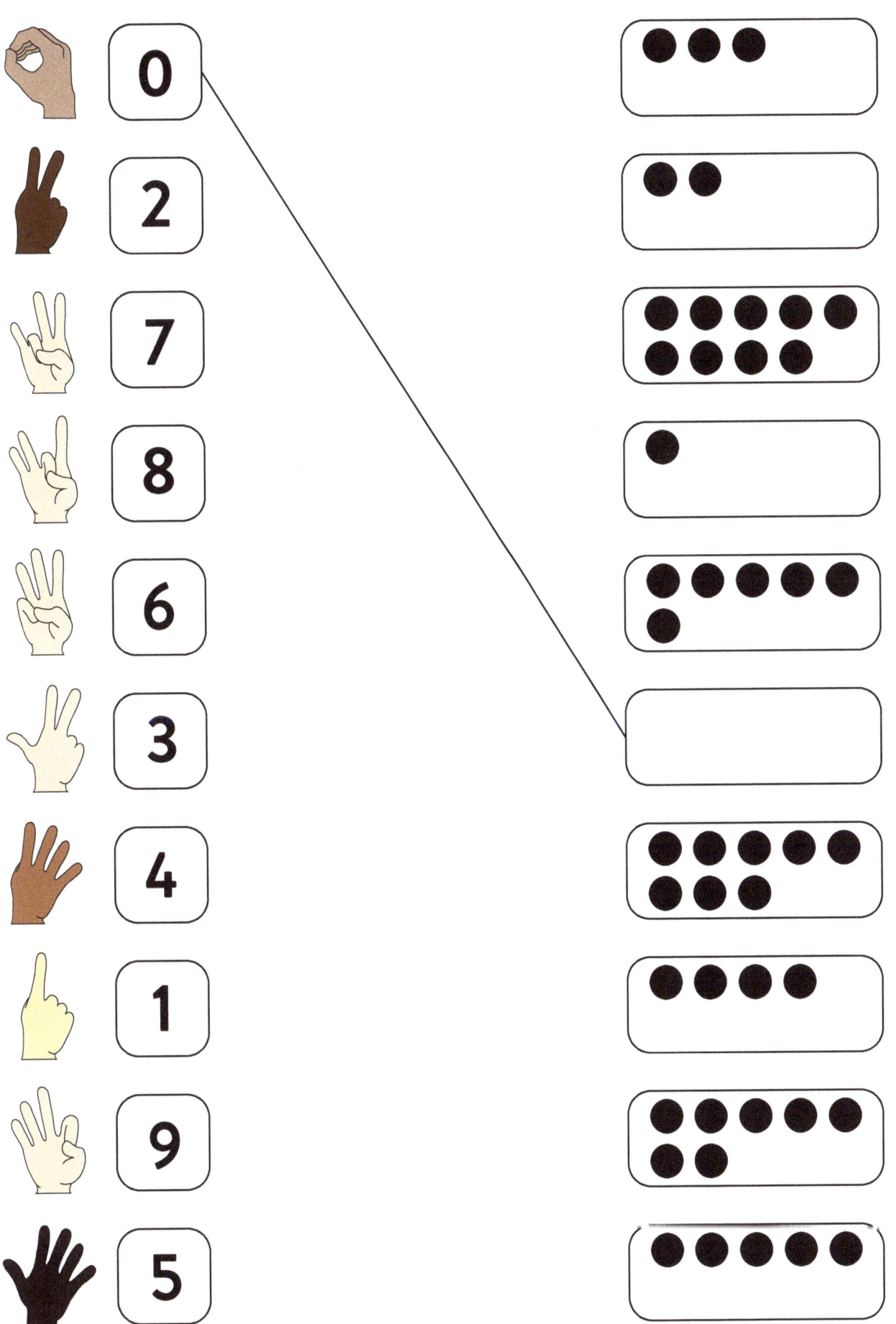

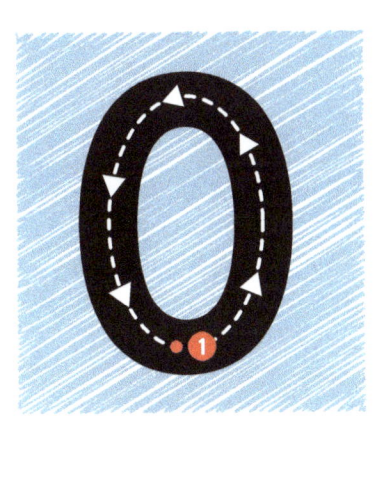  

Check some of my other books at:
www.amazon.com/author/kellelima

Scan this code with your phone!

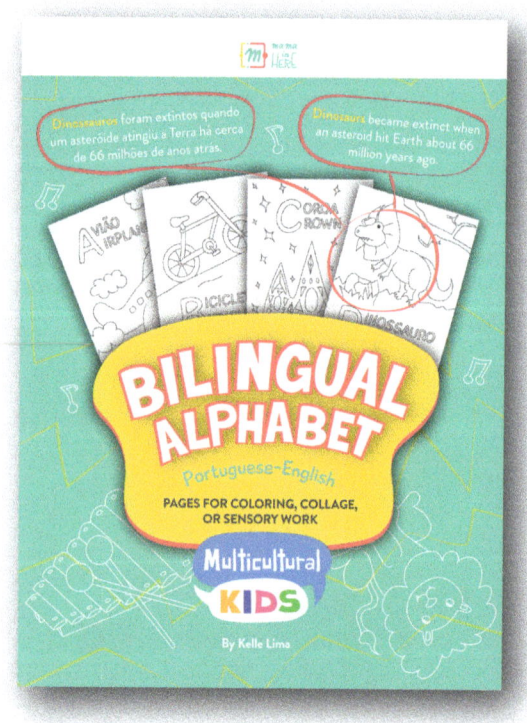

Hi there, I hope your learning journey has been great!
Did you enjoy this book?
Please consider leaving a positive review!

I would love to connect with you:

  @mamaishere2021

For FREE learning video resources, subscribe to my channel:

 bit.ly/Mamaishere

www.ingramcontent.com/pod-product-compliance
Lightning Source LLC
Chambersburg PA
CBHW041526120626

46551CB00018B/2590